Cinderella 2020

(Written by Dr. Purvi Kothari)

2021

ISBN # 978-81-951087-3-2

Dr. Purvi Kothari
Hon. Tech. Advisor. - The Orator's Hub,
327, Rajhans Ornate,
Parle Point, Surat - 395007

Publication
Nexus Stories Publication, Surat (Gujarat), Bhārata
https://nexus-stories.com
+91 87800 80718

NEXUS STORIES PUBLICATION

Surat, Gujarat, India.

First Published by Nexus Stories 2021

ISBN # 978-81-951087-3-2

CINDERELLA 2020

FROM FANTASY TO REALITY

Dr. Purvi Kothari

Author's Desk

Dear parents,

We grew up reading stories of the fantasy world in our childhood days. Our children today too, know these dreamy stories which talks about fairy land and God Mother with a magic stick.

Is it not necessary that along with the illusionary world, kids today know about the real world too, which has a flavour of reality with happiness combined with surprises with a practical preview. This book Cinderella 2020 is one such attempt made by me, Dr. Purvi Kothari to enlighten the minds of these saplings and to open the vistas of their thinking and give them vision for tomorrow. So dear parents, read with your child, connect with your child at bed time and celebrate their growth through the vision of the author. Let's believe in reality, let's believe in surprises and have faith in ourself, that, "We are the one's to create our magic ".

"Piti petti peter pool,
Life is so beautiful and cool,
All shall have their dreams and boons,
So shall fairy Godmother grant you your desired boon".

Foreword

Shri Yazdi Naoshriwan Karanjia,
Padmashri Awardee,
Renowned Parsi Theatre artist, Educationalist,
Author, Director of The Cambay Institute of Commerce and
a Social Entrepreneur and Activist.

"કાગળ, સહી સહુ ખર્ચાય જાય
ત્યારે મનનાં વિચાર, કલમે, મનમાં કોતરાય જાય"

ખરેખર દીકરા પૂર્વી, ખૂબ સરસ વાર્તા જે આજના જમાનાને અનુરૂપ છે. આજે બાળકો એટલા સોશીયલ મીડિયાંને Exposed છે કે તે આ નાજુક મન પર આડ અસર કરે છે. બાહરી સૌંદર્યથી લોભાય કેટલાય બાળકોનું ભવિષ્ય બગડે છે...Cinderella ની વાર્તાને નવો વળાંક આપી આજના બાળકોને એક નવો રસ્તો ચીંધ્યો છે. એક દિશા બતાવી છે કે જ્ઞાન, આંતરીક સુંદરતા અને ભણતર વ્યક્તિને સુંદર બનાવે છે.

Dr. Purvi, the story is simple, with the flavour of modern times and with a lovely message. I am sure every young reader will feel connected when they read this story. Keep writing and keep touching young lives....

- Yazdi

Foreword

Dr. Swati Popat Vats,
President of Podar Education Network and Early Childhood Association, India.
Founder Director of Podar Jumbo Kids and Podar Institute of Education. An eminent author, Orator and a Parenting mentor.

Cinderella brings to mind a ball, glass slippers and a girl waiting for her prince charming. This story of Cinderella 2020 written by Dr. Purvi Kothari shows children a new perspective of a different age Cinderella.

Dr. Purvi has sensitively addressed the topic of death of a parent, a step mother and having 'average' looks. This story is a must read for children in the age group of 7 and above as it is at that age that their looks in comparison to their peers becomes a topic of interest and can lead to issues like low self-esteem and even bullying.

Dr. Purvi has handled all these important issues with sensitivity and used the teaching maxim of 'known to unknown', as children know the story of Cinderella but are still learning about the emotional issues like death, relationships and understandings themselves. It is so important to ensure that our children, both boys and girls grow up reading stories that help understand 'big' emotions and are exposed to gender neutral situations and role models.

I congratulate Dr. Purvi for writing this much needed story that is a perfect example of teaching about life and life skills through a story. A must read for parents and teachers too. I wish Dr. Purvi the very best for all her future work, keep inspiring us.

Warm Regards,
Dr. Swati Popat Vats
President, Early Childhood Association
Association for Primary Education and Research

Foreword

Mrs. Maharukh Chichgar,
Renowned Theatre artist, Author, Mesmerizing Orator, Educationalist, Academician and an Iconic personality.

The story Cinderella 2020 is remarkably penned down by Dr. Purvi. This story is just about the confusion that goes on in the minds of many children. Everyone gives so much importance to outer appearance, that they forget that it is one's inner beauty that shows the real you. So, children start giving importance to outer beauty. The Cinderella we grew up reading was satisfied with glittering clothes and a handsome prince. But, Dr. Purvi tries to instil in today's children that the most important thing in life is not only grooming your outer appearance, but also developing your intellect which stays with you forever. In this story Cinderella's confusion in selecting the boon and the battle which goes on in her mind shall make children realize that truly many of them face such situations where they need to take such befitting and right decisions which may prove to be the turning point in their life.

I have seen Purvi as a quiet child sitting with plaited hair on a bench in my class. Then after years, I saw her teaching in a college. I have witnessed her pursuing her goal and working hard to get her doctorate. Yes, she went ahead in the right direction developing her intellect – but unlike Cinderella 2020, she was and still is not only beautiful in looks but even from within which reflects in her writing.

This book shall truly inspire many children to take right decisions in their life…. So, go ahead, read the book and Dr. Purvi, go ahead and write many more such books……

Warmth and love,
Maharukh Chichgar

Foreword

Amarjyotiba Gohil
Founder and Director of ASIS group, Amarjyoti Saraswati International school, Amarjyoti Saraswati Vidyalaya, Amarjyoti Saraswati pre- primary school, Silver bells public school.

Outer beauty is undoubtedly pleasing to the eyes and will grab the attention of the people. But this is transient and will fade away with time. It is the inner beauty that is infinite and adds integrity to life. Beauty consists in the strength of character. You may be judged by the harsh world in the process of proving your worth. People may or may not support you. But believing in yourself and believing in what you have thought for yourself and achieving it will certainly have an everlasting impact in the minds and hearts of people. When you believe in yourself, you can overcome self-doubt and have the confidence to take action and get things done. It does not matter what you are born with. But what you live with and what you leave behind for people to remember and get inspired is what matters.

All words of appreciation and love for Dr. Purvi kothari to have given a new perspective to the story.

Regards,
Amarjyotiba Gohil

Once upon a time in a small town in India, lived a close knit contended nuclear family.

Father Cindhu and mother Rebella found immense happiness in their cute little eight-year-old girl, Cinderella. Cinderella was the cutest, chirpiest child with curly hair and wheatish glowing skin. She was far too innocent a child with a noble heart.

Yet, a question always disturbed her. She often asked her parents, "Why did you name me Cinderella? When I am not as beautiful as a princess character as in the fairy tale!!!!"

With a blissful smile, father Cindhu would reply, "My love, look through my heart!! For us, you are the prettiest princess in the world, the sweetest and the kindest human and so there can be no other name more befitting you then Cinderella!!!

You are a blessing of love and that is why your name is a combination of our names, Cindhu and Rebella.

But as all good times end, so did the happy times of this family lapse. Mother Rebella was diagnosed with an irrecoverable stage of cancer and she passed away within a short tenure of six months.

Tears flowed from Cinderella's eyes and her heart could not take the pain, for her emotions and attachment for departed mother was beyond expression. The loss was irreparable and Cinderella could not take the setback and overcome the grief.

She could not believe that her mother was no longer with her by her side to hold her tiny fingers and cuddle her with warmth.

On the other hand, father Cindhu started struggling with daily chores.

He thought within, "If I shall not bridge the gap and bring a new mother for Cinderella, she will never be able to recover from the agony. Also, who shall feed her? Who shall send her to school?? Take care of her when I go to office??"

Cindhu was extremely worried and concerned for Cinderella.

With all these endless thoughts in mind finally Cindhu decided to remarry a widow, Kamini, who stepped in Cindhu's and Cinderella's life with her two daughters, Kanak and Kanika.

Both the daughters of mother Kamini were very pretty looking, just like their mother Kamini. Fair toned, glowing skin, golden hair, sparky eyes and all the innocence and charm which would grab every one's attention.

Cinderella was paranoid and sceptical about a new woman being introduced as a mother and that too a stepmother with siblings!!!

She had read in stories about the torture, the strictness, the discrimination that a step mother would always make to the adopted child.

But realistic relations are not always as depicted in fairy tales.

Kamini was a very well- educated lady who was a celebrated teacher in school. She was a very calm, composed, cheerful, matured lady with a humble heart. She whole heartedly accepted Cinderella as her third daughter.

It took Cinderella a few months to come out of the misconception and the scary image of a step mother and accept her mom, Kamini, with her two new readymade beautiful sisters.

As time passed by, they made a composed loving family and three girls started sharing and caring for each other.

However, there was something disturbing and boiling deep within the mind of Cinderella. Initially she did not realise but slowly and gradually she developed inferiority complex for her looks, in comparison with her two beautiful pretty sisters, Kanak and Kanika.

Whenever and wherever they would go, Kanak and Kanika would grab everyone's attention with their pretty faces.

Cinderella would feel low, would feel left out and even unrecognized, just because of her skin tone. As time passed by, the low feeling started penetrating deep within her mind, which no one realized. Slowly Cinderella started withdrawing herself from the crowd. She avoided all gatherings and festive celebrations.

Soon, Diwali approached and Cindhu's office threw a lavish party to celebrate this great Indian occasion.

The whole family dressed ethnically for the party but Cinderella denied under the pretext of being unwell. For sure, she was avoiding to go as she had developed an inferiority complex that she was not as pleasing and charming as her sisters.

Somehow, she convinced her father that she needed rest and so should stay back home. With a heavy heart and a plastic smile, the family headed for the flamboyant Diwali gathering.

That night Cinderella lay in her bed in tears, missing mom Rebella. "Why do I look so ordinary? Why am I not pretty as my sisters??? Why God has not made me as beautiful as a princess to grab everybody's attention ???"

As tears rolled down on the pillow continuously, she got exhausted. Finally, she grabbed a story book and fell asleep reading it.

And guess who came in her dream??? It was a fairy Godmother!!!

A beam of light sparkled in her room and fairy Godmother dressed in a splendid gown, holding a magic stick entered the room. Fairy Godmother asked Cinderella, "My dear girl, why didn't you go for the party?".

"Piti petti peter pool,
Life is so beautiful and cool,
All shall have their dreams and boons,
so shall fairy Godmother grant you
your desired boon".

Cinderella started weeping bitterly and poured out her heart, "Oh! I am not very pretty looking!! Neither am I that attractive, nor am I desirable." Tell me fairy Godmother, why should I go for the party?"

With a divine blush on the face, fairy Godmother replied, "Fine Cinderella, today because you have opened your heart before me, I give you two choices!!!"

You can choose to become the most beautiful girl as an attractive pleasing princess, sacrificing the goodness of heart and nobleness of thoughts or you can be blessed with immense knowledge, compassion and vigour to deal with life.

"The choice is yours!!!" announced fairy Godmother.

After vicious battle in mind and the temptation to look as charming as a princess, she churned her thoughts, "If I shall not be mature, knowledgeable, disciplined to make a challenging career, how shall beauty grace me? Good looks shall be worthless if I choose beauty over virtues!!!

Though her heart did not agree, her mind stressed upon the second option and so she asked the fairy God mother to bless her with the boon of knowledge enhancement. A boon to be brainy, hardworking, sincere and disciplined to carve out a profound career, which would make all proud.

So may it be, said the fairy Godmother and swirled the magic stick with mesmerizing words, with these words Godmother blessed Cinderella and vanished. Cinderella slept peacefully through the night with a contended smile.

SCHOOL

When she woke up the next day morning she could not believe, "Was it a dream or was I really blessed by the Godmother?"

Having believed that she was blessed by the Godmother, from that very day a sort of spirit and energy evolved within her and she thought of giving her best in her studies as she was granted a boon. She transmitted all her energies from trying to look glamorous to constructing the foundation of a substantial career.

She engraved in her heart, "Now that the Godmother has already blessed me, I need to be as the blessing goes!!!"

So, she started investing her effort in studies, sketching an identity, searching for knowledge, reading books, excavating, experimenting and discovering new things.

As she grew up and entered the college life, she faced the same critics, "Your name does not match with your looks Cinderella!! A princess with a dark skin and curly hair!!!"

Hahaha, and there was laughter all around.

By now Cinderella was used to the judgemental and biased attitude to her skin colour and she ignored the comments.

She knew she was meant for a purpose and not be the Cinderella of the fairy-tale, waiting for the magic and prince charming to lighten up her life.

Everyone laughed and poked fun at her in college, but she ignored them all. With immense determination and hard work, she finally decided to join the Indian Air force.

With all the focus and determination, she positively plunged towards pursuing her dream.

She kept working harder and harder, reaffirming faith that she was already blessed by the God mother and she was destined to make a career. She was fated to make a mark by her unique virtues and acts.

Annual Award
Function

She worked insanely hard with passion and resolution to crack the exams and become an Air force officer.

And then came the big day which was the Annual day, where the meritorious cadet was to be announced and honoured.

And finally roared the announcement Cinderella was waiting for, "And the best cadet award goes to .... Cinderella!!!" And as she stepped forward to accept the trophy, she saw all the pretty, beautiful, chirpy faces sitting in the audience, clapping for her, participating in her achievement. Cinderella thought within, "Finally I have achieved my ambition and earned recognition.

As she stood on the podium, she fondly remembered Rebella and of course the God mother who had granted her a boon, which had come true.

As her family, friends and all in the audience applauded for her she felt immensely proud.

Over whelmed, she had nothing more to say but just proudly flaunt about and admit, "Fairy Godmother, I don't know whether you really blessed me, but today I made your words come true. I hope I have made everybody proud, for Cinderella 2020 has come out of the dreamy world to achieve her desired goal."

As soon as she stepped down after her address from the podium, a suited young handsome business man walked towards her. He bent down on his knees and proposed her amidst the flooded auditorium. "You are the Cinderella I was looking for!! A bold, humble, focused women, with matured thoughts and clear vision." Will you be my life partner and complete my life?? asked the young man.

Just Married

Cinderella could not believe what was happening on the grand stage of the annual day where in thousands of people were witnessing the event. All seemed as scene of a fairy tale. Cinderella blushed and replied, "Today is a big day for me. It is a day where in my inner beauty has been accepted and me as Cinderella of 2020."

The story goes on as she marries the young charming man and accepts him as a life partner with a belief that in 2020 too, magic does happen and dreams do come true.

MORAL

Life is full of happiness and surprises, only if we learn to accept and honour what has been bestowed upon us!!!!

Game : Help Cinderella achieve her dream

Rule : You can trace just once. Carefully help her to reach her dream.

Game: Join the dots and Color Cinderella

Game : Word Search Puzzle

Q	K	H	V	A	M	B	G	X	L
K	A	J	N	D	I	P	T	R	W
C	N	K	P	O	O	L	O	Y	U
A	I	A	I	R	F	O	R	C	E
N	K	N	V	K	H	F	C	H	L
C	A	A	D	A	S	F	D	C	M
E	L	K	R	H	T	N	X	B	Q
R	N	O	Y	W	U	Y	B	L	F

1. What is the name of Cinderella's father?
2. Cinderella's mother died of _ .
3. What is the name of Cinderella's stepsisters?
4. Piti Petti Peter _
5. Cinderella became an _ officer.

DO YOU KNOW WHO INVENTED CINDERELLA???

For sure, Disney didn't invent Cinderella, for her birth was 2000 years prior.

So dear ones, Cinderella has been a part of our childhood memory which brings afresh a dreamy character which imbibes in us morals and values as honesty, purity and serenity. Cinderella never knew, she was destined to be a princess. Yet, her noble gestures made her the queen of hearts.

So as soon as we talk about Cinderella, what comes to our mind??? It's the wicked stepmother, stepsisters, fairy godmother and a handsome prince who fell in love with her before the clock struck 12. But that's not the real Cinderella. It's the one pictured by Disney works, which animated the film and portrayed her in theatres in 1950's.

THEN WHEN WAS EXACTLY CINDERELLA BORN??? THE FIRST CINDERELLA WAS GREEK:

The European folktale evolved Cinderella as a girl in big blue ball gown with a century old plot that has passed through cultures for a millennium. In the first ancient story, which dates back to 6th century BC in Greek history, a Greek courtesan named Rhodophis, had one of her shoes stolen by an eagle who flew with it across Mediterranean and dropped it in the lap of an Egyptian king. Taking the shoe as a sign from heaven, the king went on a quest to find the owner of the shoe. When he found Rhodophis he married her, lifting her from the low status to the throne.

THE EUROPEAN CENRENTOLA:

More than 500 versions of Cinderella story have been found just in Europe. The European version of the story originated in the 17th century, when a story called Cenerentola was published in a collection of Italian short stories. Cenerentola had all the ingredients of the olden tale – The wicked stepmother, stepsister, magic wand, missing slipper and all the miracle.

THE FRENCH CENDRILLON:

6 years later, this story took a French twist and got shape of the story we know today. A French writer Charles Perrault invented the fairy-tale, Cendrillon, Cinderella as we know today for all the years to come.

THE FINAL CINDERELLA:

Finally, Disney works sketched, pictured and animated Cinderella as a film which continues to live in our hearts and minds even today.

WHAT KIDS NEED TO UNDERSTAND??

DID CINDERELLA INVENT THE WICKED STEPMOTHER TREND????

"NO"

Many fairy tales of the 17th century as snow-white, Hansel and Gretel, had featured evil stepmother who ruined stepdaughter's life. In all these stories the stepmother remained the enemy of the stepdaughter, leaving a dirty image of the husband's second marriage. This took a wicked shape in the societal mind where stepmothers till date are signalled for bad treatment, less proximity and discrimination towards the stepchild. These stories have created a stereotype image of a stepmother which brings a disillusioned figure of acceptance even today in a child's mind.

TODAY'S FRESH PERSPECTIVE FOR CHILDREN:

"Gone are the days when marriage was a life-long deal. It's OK in today's times to remarry and have a compatible life partner. With these changes, the age-old wicked portrayal of a stepmother should also change. Children need to accept new members with love and positivity.

CINDERELLA IS A STORY ABOUT CLASS WARFARE:

At its core Cinderella is about how dependent women once were on men to determine their place in the world. Each story of Cinderella has portrayed an upper middle-class girl on the mercy of her stepmother who is deprived of love and luxury. However, in the changing scenario and social environment these taboos need to be revived.

Cinderella 2020 pitches today's preview where children should have broader vision and acceptance towards a new family system. Also, the Cinderella of today has become independent and makes the man in her life a choice and not a compulsion.

CHEERS TO THE CINDERELLA OF 2020

Cinderella 2020 is a story of a cute little girl with simple looks. She grows up desiring to be a beautiful princess but realises her worth in creating her identity. She is Cinderella of today who is composed, matured and believes in carving out her career instead of waiting for prince charming to make her happy.

The story erases many myths and misconceptions and provides a dynamic thinking to the reader, which is the need of the hour.

About the Author

Dr Purvi Kothari is a Professor at Sir. K. P. College of Commerce, Surat, with an enriched academic experience of 24 yrs. As a doctor in Social Marketing, she has written and published exceeding 50 research papers on varied subjects of management and finance, in reputed journals and won many " Best Research Paper" awards. She has been conferred with Shikshan Ratna Award for her excellence in teaching and service by the Sarvajanik Education Society.

Apart from academic achievements, she is a celebrated author for kids' book, " Rooting thoughts", an impactful orator, certificated career counsellor and a research guide. She has written number of reference books for UG and PG students as Indian Financial Markets, Marketing mantras, Financial Planning through Mutual Funds, Social Marketing and many more in the pipeline. She is recognised for her affiliation with Chamber of Commerce, SMC and numerous noble charitable organisations. She has served as a resource person at reputed colleges and conferences and as guest speaker at National and International levels.

*****